It Is Fu...

by Michelle Lawrence   illustrated by Julia Gorton

Orlando   Boston   Dallas   Chicago   San Diego

Visit *The Learning Site!*

www.harcourtschool.com

Printed in China

ISBN 0-15-325436-X

8 9 10 121 10 09 08 07 06 05 04

Ordering Options
ISBN 0-15-323766-X (Collection)
ISBN 0-15-329608-9 (package of 5)

Come on, Sam.
It is fun here.

I like it a lot.

I do not like it, Pam.
It is not fun.

Look at the bug, Sam.
See, it is fun.

I do not like it, Pam.
It is not fun.

Look at the net, Sam.
See, it is fun.

I do not like it, Pam.
It is not fun.

I like it, Pam.
It is fun here.